Samuel French Acting Edition

Poe's Midnight Dreary

by Richard McElvain

SAMUELFRENCH.COM   SAMUELFRENCH.CO.UK

Copyright © 1991 by Richard McElvain
All Rights Reserved

POE'S MIDNIGHT DREARY is fully protected under the copyright laws of the United States of America, the British Commonwealth, including Canada, and all other countries of the Copyright Union. All rights, including professional and amateur stage productions, recitation, lecturing, public reading, motion picture, radio broadcasting, television and the rights of translation into foreign languages are strictly reserved.

ISBN 978-0-874-40682-5

www.SamuelFrench.com
www.SamuelFrench.co.uk

For Production Enquiries

United States and Canada
Info@SamuelFrench.com
1-866-598-8449

United Kingdom and Europe
Plays@SamuelFrench.co.uk
020-7255-4302

Each title is subject to availability from Samuel French, depending upon country of performance. Please be aware that *POE'S MIDNIGHT DREARY* may not be licensed by Samuel French in your territory. Professional and amateur producers should contact the nearest Samuel French office or licensing partner to verify availability.

CAUTION: Professional and amateur producers are hereby warned that *POE'S MIDNIGHT DREARY* is subject to a licensing fee. Publication of this play(s) does not imply availability for performance. Both amateurs and professionals considering a production are strongly advised to apply to Samuel French before starting rehearsals, advertising, or booking a theatre. A licensing fee must be paid whether the title(s) is presented for charity or gain and whether or not admission is charged. Professional/Stock licensing fees are quoted upon application to Samuel French.

No one shall make any changes in this title(s) for the purpose of production. No part of this book may be reproduced, stored in a retrieval system, or transmitted in any form, by any means, now known or yet to be invented, including mechanical, electronic, photocopying, recording, videotaping, or otherwise, without the prior written permission of the publisher. No one shall upload this title(s), or part of this title(s), to any social media websites.

For all enquiries regarding motion picture, television, and other media rights, please contact Samuel French.

MUSIC USE NOTE

Licensees are solely responsible for obtaining formal written permission from copyright owners to use copyrighted music in the performance of this play and are strongly cautioned to do so. If no such permission is obtained by the licensee, then the licensee must use only original music that the licensee owns and controls. Licensees are solely responsible and liable for all music clearances and shall indemnify the copyright owners of the play(s) and their licensing agent, Samuel French, against any costs, expenses, losses and liabilities arising from the use of music by licensees. Please contact the appropriate music licensing authority in your territory for the rights to any incidental music.

IMPORTANT BILLING AND CREDIT REQUIREMENTS

If you have obtained performance rights to this title, please refer to your licensing agreement for important billing and credit requirements.

NOTE TO THE READER

What follows are some notes about this play which can be staged with a sprawling high-tech fat budget set with a cast of thousands or quite simply with a few platforms and flats and six to eight actors. Included with the text is a suggestion of a set and suggestions for staging actors on that set. They are here only as a point of reference and you, the director, may exploit or disregard them as you see fit.

The text includes numbered footnotes to illustrate how certain theatrical devices might be realized—again to be enjoyed or ignored.

At first reading the play might seem male heavy, but I would encourage you to resist that seeming. Roles like Moran, Bertram, Allouisius, the cat, etc. could be played by women. Also, roles like Allen or Zachary or Poe himself could be played by women in drag which would not be inconsistent with Poe's off center view of the world.

The play does not require quite as complex a set as I have sketched—any simpler more theatrical design devices you might invent, I feel would only enhance the effect of the show.

I would encourage you to take liberties with the "Chorus." What is sketched in the script is a small cast with 1, 2, 3, and 4 roughly divided into soprano (1), tenor (2), mezzo (3), and baritone/bass (4) vocal ranges. It could be done with four, eight or forty eight voices (wouldn't that be fun!). And as you work you might want to redistribute them as the "music" of the voices of your production develop regardless of tonal range. (All choral lines could conceivably be done by one actor.)

ACT I

Scene 1

(Night. Sound of a THUNDERSTORM held at bay by several systems of doors. We see the flash of LIGHT through the window of the doors. Then the faint but insistent TAPPING on the door.)

POE. *(Whispered—perhaps on tape.)*
Once upon a midnight dreary while I pondered weak and weary,
Over many a quaint and curious volume of forgotten lore,
While I nodded nearly napping suddenly there came ... a tapping!

(Live tapping on UC door. Continues faint slow, insistent.)

POE.
As of someone gently rapping, rapping at my chamber door.
    CHORUS[1]. *(Stand flanking set—whispered.)* "Tis some visitor"
    POE. I muttered.
    CHORUS.
"Tapping at my chamber door—
       Only this and nothing more"

(Pause, STORM still muffled—TAPPING—faint, slow, insistent.)

POE.
And the silken sad uncertain rustling of each purple curtain
Troubled me—filled me with fantastic
Terrors never felt before.
So that now, to still the beating of my heart, I stood repeating,
    POE & CHORUS (2), (1). *(Vocal crescendo.)* Is some
visitor entreating entrance to my chamber door
POE & CHORUS (1), (2), (3). Some late visitor entreating
entrance at my chamber door—
    POE & CHORUS. *(Forte.)* This is it and nothing more.

(TAPPING has grown louder and at chorus's last word doors burst open. Two PEOPLE carry POE—delirious, screaming at the top of his lungs, through $\underline{A}$ to $\underline{D}$.* STORM rages behind.)

PERSON 1. Nurse!, Nurse! *(Over his screams.)*
NURSE. *(Cross to $\underline{D}$.)* Yes.
PERSON 2. A doctor quickly.

(SHE signals another nurse from opposite flank who wheels on "bed"^{2}—to $\underline{D}$, foot of bed U. Doors are closed—sounds of STORM once again at bay. POE is placed on "bed" head hangs off D. still wailing.)

NURSE. Have him bite on this—*(NURSE 2 places leather board in mouth as others "tie" him down. The leather board reduces the wails but POE continues to thrash in his fit.)* Who is he?

---

* See ground plan.

PERSON 1. We don't know.
PERSON 2. We found him like this writhing in the gutter.
NURSE. Fetch Dr. Moran. Tell him it's an emergency.

(MEN 1 and 2 exit. NURSES silently U. of him. SPOT up on DR. MORAN D.at E)

MORAN. This is as faithful an account as I am able to furnish for the record of the Death of one Edgar A. Poe. My name is John T. Moran, Washington College Hospital, Baltimore, Wednesday Oct 3, 1849. *(Crosses up to Poe D— removes leather board—POE babbles words incomprehensibly.)* Brought here unconscious but delirious and violent. He remained in this condition for ten hours. *(POE is now less violent—but trembles and babbles under Dr. Moran.)* To this state succeeded tremor of the limbs and at first a busy but not violent or active delirium—constant talking.

(POE starts seeing title[3] El Dorado perhaps above him.)

POE. Ahhh!
MORAN. And a vacant converse with spectral and imaginary objects on the walls.

(Title appears to audience—"EL DORADO.")

POE. *(Pointing to title.)* Ahh, Ahhh!
NURSE. Shhh! There's nothing there.
POE. *(Protesting.)* No No. Do-ra. Do—El—*(Finding the words under Moran.)*
NURSE, NURSE, DOC. Shhhhhhhh *(ALL freeze.)*

(POE sits, than stands from their freeze, ropes fall off.
As POE recites El Dorado, NURSES and DOCTORS exit in
 slow motion w/bed. Eerie MUSIC.)

    POE.
Gaily bedlight,
A gallant knight, *(Indicates himself.)*
In sunshine and in shadow,
Had Journeyed long,
Singing a song,
In search of Eldorado.

(CHARACTERS walk in dream-like; BERTRAM with
 cleaver, ZACHARY with ax, VIRGINIA, ALLEN, cat
 with eye patch, PALLAS, etc. THEY create a tableau
 around Poe, still at D.)

    POE.
But he grew old—
This knight so bold—
And o'er his heart a shadow
Fell, as he found
No spot of ground
That looked like Eldorado.

And, as his strength
Failed him at length,
He met a pilgrim shadow—
"Shadow," said he,
"Where can it be—
This land of Eldorado?"

CHARACTERS. *(Whispered.)*
"Over the Mountains
Of the Moon,
Down the Valley of the Shadow,
Ride, boldly ride,"
    POE.
The shade replied,—
    CHARACTERS.
"If you seek for Eldorado!"
    POE. *(Searchingly, looks around, sees he is free—alone with his creations, solemn. MUSIC out, gesturing to characters.)*
I am in a dream land—
Where dwell the ghouls—
By each spot the most unholy—
In each nook most melancholy
There the traveler meets a ghost
Sheeted memories of the Past—
Shrouded forms that start and sigh
As they pass the wanderer by—
White robed forms of friends long given,
In agony, to the Earth—

(At E pool of LIGHT, enter ALLEN. HE laughs, rudely.)

    POE.
and Heaven.

(At G, pool of LIGHT, enter VIRGINIA.)

    VIRGINIA. Eddy ...
    POE. Virginia ... come with me, I ...

(HE goes toward her but is interrupted by CHEERS and APPLAUSE, CHARACTERS turn U., cross to C facing U., each removes or hides elements of characters—cleaver, masks, etc. POE is drawn to participate in the crowd. VIRGINIA exits and a cheering CROWD draws around ALLEN who magnanimously accepts their attention. HE continues his parlor performance of bawlderdized Shakespeare. Perhaps he has a Scottish accent. His performance is punctuated with crowd responses of CHEERS, APPLAUSE and LAUGHTER. HE is not drunk, but aglow with drink)

ALLEN. *(At C facing crowd area 3.)* Once more unto the breach dear friends once more; *(APPLAUSE.)* Or close the damn wall with our English and Scottish *(CHEER.)* dead! In peace there's nothing so becomes a man as modest stillness and humility. But when the bloody blast of war blows in our ears, then imitate the action ... of the tiger—Grrr. *(Which HE personifies to CHEERS.)* I see you stand like greyhounds in the slips, straining upon the start. The game's afoot. Follow your spirit and upon this charge try—God for Harry! Britain, St. George and Blessed Mary the Queen!! *(Loud CHEERS and APPLAUSE. CROWD gathers around him on C. HE mills and chats.)*

POE. *(Now a young boy running to Allen at C but does not mount platform.)* Papa, Papa, that was thrilling.

ALLEN. Away Boy—later. *(Turning to someone.)* Horace, I want to ...

POE. But Papa you promised too ... *(Reaching, pulling on him.)*

ALLEN. *(Pushing him off.)* I said *Not Now* boy.

POE. But Father you ...

ALLEN. *(Angered.)* ... and don't call me your father ...

POE. *(CROWD silences at outburst—deeply embarrassing the young POE who begins to cry.)* But Father ...

ALLEN. I'm not your father.

POE. But I ...

ALLEN. Can you get that in your thick little bastard's skull, you are not my son. *(Turns back to crowd.)*

POE. Please ... *(Finding alternative name.)* ... Mr. Allen.

ALLEN. Get out of here now, I have guests to attend to. *(Kicking him away—rekindling the party.)* Come Johnny, Maggie ... *(THEY turn their backs to Poe and continue "party" facing U. as POE scrambles to writing desk.)*

POE. *(The young man again.)* To John Allen—March 19, 1837.

ALLEN. *(To guests.)* I've been guardian to the bastard for twenty years ...

(CROWD ad-lib mocking responses.)

POE. *(Fetching "writing desk"[4] at G, he is now a young man.)* After my treatment on yesterday and what passed between us this morning, I can hardly think you will be surprised at the contents of this letter. *(Laughter bursts from the party—subsides.)* My determination is at length taken to leave your house and endeavor to find some place in this wide world where I will be treated not as you have treated me.

ALLEN. *(Turning and crying.)* Go on Eddy—Get out, Ha! find "a place for yourself in this wide world." Ha! *(Turns back to crowd.)*

POE. My resolution is unalterable ...

ALLEN. What are you going to do? Live off your poems?! Ha! Wastrel!

POE. I beseech you, send me my trunk containing my clothes and books.

ALLEN. What!?

POE. ... and as much money as will defray the expenses of my passage to some of the northern cities and then support me for one month ...

ALLEN. Never.

POE. By which time I shall be enabled to place myself in some situation ...

ALLEN. Situation Ha! Never. Never more.

(Title appears.)

"THE TELLTALE HEART"

(Party LAUGHTER builds and transforms into the WAILS of inmates in a mad house, as party breaks up and exits, BERTRAM is taken by keeper to B. BERTRAM is chained in place in his cell, at E, as POE writes ...)

POE. It is impossible.

(KEEPER paces off platform near B.)

POE &BERTRAM. To say how first the idea entered my brain.

BERTRAM. True!—nervous—very very dreadfully nervous. I had been ... and am, but why *will* you say that I am mad? The disease had sharpened my senses—not destroyed—not dulled them. Above all was my sense of hearing acute.

Harken ... *(HE launches forward to tell us his story but is restrained by wrist cuffs[5] strikes B violently, BERTRAM retreats in fear. POE exits with desk. KEEPER paces past DF thumping a club in his palm as a warning—then exits.)* Observe how calmly—how healthfully I can tell the story. *(LIGHTS—big change larger DS area D is lit in cool bath of light. BERTRAM free to talk & tell his story sheds his chains. [Note: there is no need to "act" crazy because of the set up. He should seem innocent & charming.])* It is impossible to say how first the idea entered my brain; but once conceived it haunted me day and night. He had never wronged me. *(Enter—charming REGINALD with cane, eye patch, book. Crosses to bed which has rolled in D. to E. [Actor who plays Allen also plays Reginald.])*

REGINALD. Good evening Bertram.

BERTRAM. Sir, you're looking well this evening.

REGINALD. Thank you Bertram. *(Goes to bed and begins settling down.)*

BERTRAM. He had never given me insult. For his gold, I had no desire. I think it was his eye! *(REGINALD—back to us—removes eye patch, perhaps projection of eye appears—SOUND EFFECT—grotesque.)* Yes, it was this. One of his eyes resembled that of a ... of a ... vulture—a pale blue eye with a film over it. Whenever it fell upon me ...

REGINALD. Bertram!? *(Looking at* Bertram.*)*

BERTRAM. My blood ran cold! Yes sir.

REGINALD. Could you take this for me?

BERTRAM. Right away sir. *(Crosses D. to E to him in revulsion and brings book and cane away to D.)* ... and so by degrees—very—gradually—I made up my mind to take the life of the old man and thus rid myself of the eye forever. *(Rips apart book [new up charming mood.])* Now this is the point you fancy me mad. Madmen know nothing. But you should have seen me! Wisdom! Caution! Foresight! *(Whispering.) I was never kinder to the old man than during the whole week before I killed him. (Fetches lantern preset UL. of B.)* And every night, about midnight, I turned the latch of his door and opened it—oh, so gently! And then, when I had made an opening sufficient for my head, I put in a dark lantern, all close, closed, so than no light shone out, and then I thrust in my head. Oh, you would have laughed to see how cunningly I thrust it in! I moved it slowly. It took me an hour to place my whole head within the opening so far that I could see him as he lay upon his bed. Ha! —would a madman have been so wise as this? And I undid the lantern cautiously—much that a single thin ray fell upon the vulture eye. And this I did for seven long nights—every night just at midnight. But I found the eye always closed *(Eye projection fades.);* and so it was impossible to do the work; for it was not the old man who vexed me, but his evil eye. Every morning when day broke ... *(Exchange lantern for tray beside B, entering chamber at E [lighting change] with tray—"boldly.")* Your breakfast, sir.

    REGINALD. Thank you, Bertram *(Eye patch on.)*

    BERTRAM. How did you pass the night?

    REGINALD. Oh, tolerably well, passably well. Kind of you to ask.

    BERTRAM. The porridge not warm sir?

    REGINALD. Yes fine. Fine as always, not hungry that's all. *(With great affection.)* Thank heavens I have you Bertram!

    BERTRAM. *(Crossing back to B exchanges tray for lantern. LIGHT change [night] crosses toward E.)* Upon the eighth night I was more than usually cautious in opening the door. A watch's minute hand moves more quickly than did mine. *(Whispering.)* I had my head in and was about to open the lantern when ... *(Fumbles with lantern making a noise.)*

REGINALD. *(Bolting up.)* Who's there? *(Silence. Groan of mortal terror ... not a groan of pain or grief... it was the low stifled sound that arises from the bottom of the soul when overcharged with awe [silence][terrified].)* It is nothing but the wind in the chimney—it is only a mouse crossing the floor—it is merely a cricket which has made a single chirp ... yes. *(HE settles back uneasily to bed.)*

BERTRAM. *(Whispered.)* When I had waited a long time I resolved to open a very very little crevice in the lantern. A single dim ray like the thread of the spider shot from the crevice and fell upon the vulture eye *(Eye projection— SOUND.)* It was open! I grew furious—it chilled the very marrow in my bones. Now I say I could see nothing but ... *(Soft deliberate HEARTBEAT heard—it might increase in rate but not in volume.)* Now there came to my ears a low dull quick sound such as a watch makes when enveloped in cotton. It was the beating of the old man's heart. It increased my fury as the beating of a drum stimulates the soldier into courage.

(BERTRAM moves into room at E. REGINALD bolts up again. REGINALD shrieks—BERTRAM grabs him and strangles him on the U. edge of the bed. THEY struggle and end up U. behind the bed—as strangling is completed HEARTBEAT slows to a stop. BERTRAM "smiles" gaily.)

BERTRAM. Yes, he was stone dead. I placed my hand on the heart. There was no pulsation—stone dead. His eye would trouble me no more. *([At that point, actor playing REGINALD can hide beneath bed[2] and put out body parts as the dismemberment takes place.] BERTRAM speaks brightly.)* If you still think me mad, you will think so no longer when I describe the wise precautions I took for concealment of the body. *(Pulls out cleaver from inside bed[2].)* I took out some loose wall boards *(Does so on facing of platform B.)* Then I dismembered the corpse. I cut off the head ... *(Swings cleaver athletically down onto "body" U. of bed. [SOUND should be deep acoustic[6]—not synthetic—perhaps with echo.] BERTRAM takes "head"[7] and deposits it in space under platform at B.)* ... then the arms *(Crosses back to E. More cleaver work— more SOUNDS.)* ... and legs *(More cleaver— more SOUNDS, BERTRAM deposits "arms" and "legs" in U. space at B—then drags the torso in.)* There was nothing to wash out—no blood spot whatever. A tub and bucket had caught all. So clever, so cunning—no eye—not even his, could have detected anything wrong. *(As HE rolls bed off stage.)* When I had made an end of these labors it was four o'clock—still dark as midnight.

(DOORBELL [freeze! terror! slowly cross to door] at A.)

BERTRAM. Come in.

O'HERNIGAN. *(Speaks with an Irish accent.)* Sorry to disturb you, sir, at this late hour. Captain O'Hernigan, Baltimore Police.

BERTRAM. Not at all, Captain. How may I help you!

O'HERNIGAN. You would be Mr. Reginald Gustafson?

BERTRAM. No. The Master is gone on an extended trip abroad. I'm his servant. What is the problem?

O'HERNIGAN. A shriek had been heard by a neighbor during the night. A report was lodged at headquarters, and we've been dispatched to search the premises.

BERTRAM. Come in. *(CAPTAIN enters.)* I assure you everything is in order but feel free to inspect the premises.

(THEY do, crossing in to D. Silence as THEY look around. CAPTAIN notices something on the floor where "dismembering" took place—then shrugs it off—nothing. OFFICER looks carefully at the boards where they were replaced at B.)

O'HERNIGAN. Lovely woodwork in these old places.*(Motions to officer to leave.)*
BERTRAM. *(Becoming over-confident.)* Would you like to see his silver collection—locked up tight in the pantry.
O'HERNIGAN. There's no need of that, thank you.
BERTRAM. The wall safe is in the parlor if you wish to check for tampering. *(Chuckling.)*
O'HERNIGAN. That's quite all right, I ...
BERTRAM. I'm only joking. Here sit down and rest for a moment. Working so late—perhaps you would share a tankard of rum. *(Produces chairs and mugs from beside B.)*
O'HERNIGAN. *(After thinking.)* Why thank you, sir, that would be most hospitable.

(THEY sit, officer at D—BERTRAM chooses to place his chair directly before the boards where the corpse is at B— sits, leans the chair back against them smiling and drinking.)

BERTRAM. Do you often get sent on such exotic errands in the wee hours? *(Chuckles.)*

O'HERNIGAN. Ha ha. No no. It's normally quite peaceful at headquarters these times. You realize we was only doing our jobs coming here.

BERTRAM. Of course. My, I must say I am impressed. Impressed indeed. Such thoroughness is to be complimented. I'll sleep sounder tonight knowing you are out there watching the city.

O'HERNIGAN. Thank you sir *(Laughter.)*

BERTRAM. Yes yes. A criminal would have to be very fast indeed to fool you gentlemen. *(Laughter—under which the heartbeats begin softly, BERTRAM falls forward sitting upright suddenly.)*

O'HERNIGAN. Are you all right sir?

BERTRAM. Hum? I'm fine. Perfectly fine. Why do you ask? After all it is quite late. Sometimes due to fatigue and distraction you ... *(The HEART beats louder and compels him to stop.)*

O'HERNIGAN. You were saying sir ... you were ...

BERTRAM. What?

O'HERNIGAN. I was just asking ...

BERTRAM. I heard nothing you must be hearing the wind in the shutters *(Crossing to mimed window at G, BERTRAM realizes where the noise is coming from.)*

O'HERNIGAN. I didn't say I had heard a thing.

BERTRAM. *(HEART beat continues, amplifies slightly.)* I'm sorry I'm sorry I'm getting a bit of a headache I'm afraid *(Paces to E and back to G.)*—a ringing in my ears!

O'HERNIGAN. I'm sorry to hear that, perhaps I can call a doctor.

BERTRAM. Doctor. *(Laugh.)* No I'm fine. Please pay no attention to me, so tell me *(Rallying to restore his candor.)*

With a job like yours I imagine you don't often get to go to the theater.

O'HERNIGAN. To tell you the truth sir I ...

BERTRAM. *(BEATING quite loud.)* Ahh! *(Grasping his ears, discovering, aside.)* The noise is not in my ears! *(Then recovering.)* Surely they hear it—a low dull quick sound much like a watch makes when enveloped in cotton!

O'HERNIGAN. I assure you sir to my ears it's quiet as a tomb in here. *(Laughing uncomfortably.)*

BERTRAM. Ha ha of course! Is it possible you hear it not? Almighty God! No no! You heard! You hear. You suspect it. You know! You mock my horror! Ah! Louder! Louder! Louder! *Louder! (Screaming quite mad.)* Villains! Dissemble no more! I admit the deed! Look behind the panel! *(Tears off planks.)* Here here!

O'HERNIGAN. *(Looking.)* Merciful God! Heaven save us!

BERTRAM. *(HEART beat stops.)* It is the beating of his hideous heart—I killed him! I killed the vulture eye. Hear it!? *(As HE raves he is put back in shackles on B and LIGHT returns to start of section, heartbeats begin again—grow louder under his cry finally smother his calls then.)* MAKE IT STOP! THE HEART. STOP! STOP STOP STOP STOP! IT IS THE BEATING OF HIS HIDEOUS HEARTTTTTT!!!!!

(As BERTRAM screams in chains, POE is wheeled on in bed to D by nurses, wailing exactly like BERTRAM.— LIGHTS out on BERTRAM as DR. MORA enters and stands beside POE who now calms somewhat and moans. Bed is parallel to set with Poe's head R., feet L., MORAN U. of bed.)

MORAN. *(To audience.)* I was summoned to his bedside as soon as consciousness supervened and questioned him in reference to his family, place of relatives, etc. But his answers were incoherent and unsatisfactory. Wishing to rally and sustain his fast sinking hopes I told him ... *(To Poe.)* Mr. Poe?

POE. *(Weakly.)* Yes, Doctor

MORAN. In a few days you should be able to enjoy the society of your friends and I would be most happy to ...

POE. *(Bubbling towards renewed hysteria.)* Ha! Friend! Ha! Doctor are you making some rude joke?!

MORAN. Mr. Poe I'm merely ...

POE. The best thing my best friend could do would be to blow out my brains with a pistol. When I behold my degradation I am ready to sink into the earth.

MORAN. Mr. Poe if you could ...

POE. Dr. Snodgrass, you are a physician ...

MORAN. My name is Moran, Mr. Poe ...

POE. ... and I presume no physician can have difficulty in detecting the "drunkard" at a glance.

MORAN. I can't know what you ...

POE. I'm fine, I pledge you, before God, the solemn word of a gentleman, that I am temperate even to rigor. I never drank but for a brief period while I resided in Richmond, I certainly did give way at long intervals to the temptations held on all sides by the spirit of southern conviviality.

MORAN. Lie down Mr. Poe and try ...

POE. My sensitive temperament could not stand an excitement which was an everyday matter to my companions ... *(MORAN has exited. REVELERS, mardi gras, enter laughing obscenely—very drunk to C.)* In short, sometimes I was completely intoxicated. For years since I have, I have abandoned every kind of alcoholic drink ... *(FORTUNATO, a harlequin/reveler, passes a bottle to Poe at D.)* ... with the exception of a single deviation—when I was induced to resort to the occasional use of cider *(Drinks.)* with the hope of relieving a nervous attack. *(Drinks.)* Drink became my jailer. *(Approaching the harlequin.)* So I resolved to escape my prison.

FORTUNATO. Would you join me in a sip of sherry?

POE. I longed to drive it from me *(Leaves bed, crosses up to C.)*—destroy it—immolate it behind a wall of immovable stone.

FORTUNATO. It's very fine sherry—I believe it's Amontillado.

(POE smashes bottle, throws Fortunato into a nitch in wall at back of C and chains him there.)

FORTUNATO. What are you doing? Is this some joke?

(POE begins placing huge stones in front of the nitch with aid of other REVELERS, walling him in.)

POE. *(Laughs demonically.)* Yes!

(REVELERS echo his laugh as THEY wall up Fortunato under Poe's direction.)

FORTUNATO. Ha! Ha! He! He! An excellent jest indeed. We will have many a rich laugh about it, he! he! he! Over our wine—Hee! hee!

POE. The Amontillado! *(More stones in place.)*

FORTUNATO. Hee! Hee! Hee!—hee! hee! hee! Yes, the Amontillado. Will not they be awaiting us above? Let us be gone.

POE. Yes, let us be gone. *(Laughs. REVELERS exit.)*

(FORTUNATO struggles against chains as POE continues to brick him up.)

FORTUNATO. FOR THE LOVE OF GOD, LUDOVICO!

POE. Yes, for the love of God! *(Places last stone in place, faint SCREAMS heard behind wall.)* In Pace Requiescat.

(ZACHARY appears behind Poe at A.)

ZACHARY. Edgar.
POE. *(Startled.)* What—Who's there!
ZACHARY. Shhhh *(Faint MOANS behind wall.)*
POE. Who are you?
ZACHARY. *(Crossing to "new" wall at C.)* A friend, nice handy work. *(Final death MOAN.)*
POE. This is nothing, just some long overdue repair work in my cellar.
ZACHARY. Yes, very good, excellent ... you wouldn't know where I might find a pipe of Amontillado? *(MOANS behind wall.)*
POE. Get out of here! Do not mock me! Who are you?
ZACHARY. But, you do know me. Surely you remember Pluto ... our Black cat!!!

(Enter a woman as CAT—at A, tittle appears.)

"THE BLACK CAT"

POE. Nooooo!

ZACHARY. You know, from infancy I was noted for the docility and humanity of my disposition.

POE. Please, no please.

ZACHARY. I want to tell you a story. It will only take a moment. Please. Perhaps you can help me remember it?

POE. Help?

ZACHARY. Yes. After all, you created me.

POE. Go on.

ZACHARY. Thank you. *(Crossing up to A to Pluto.)* As I was telling you, my tenderness of heart was even so conspicuous as to make me the jest of my companions. *(Petting cat, cat purrs, plays.)*

POE. How well I know the feeling.

WIFE. *(Enters door at A laughing.)* Edgar. How wonderful to see you. *(SHE wears white gloves.)*

ZACHARY. Surely, you remember my wife. *(ZACHARY and WIFE are very affectionate.)*

POE. *(Terrified.)* Yes ... yes, but.

WIFE. *(Indicating cat.)* Oh you found her.

ZACHARY. Who?

WIFE. My little surprise.

ZACHARY. Oh dear, not another pet.

WIFE. But you loved them so.

ZACHARY. Yes ... All of them *(THEY laugh!)* I tell you Edgar she's turned our home into a veritable menagerie. Birds, gold fish, dogs.

WIFE. Stop my dear.

ZACHARY. Even a monkey.

WIFE. But look at her! How can you resist her.

ZACHARY. What a fine black coat. *(Pets cat.)*

POE. Be careful.

ZACHARY & WIFE. Hmm? What?

POE. It's an ancient and popular notion that all black cats are witches in disguise. *(THEY all laugh.)*

WIFE. Witches, yes. Watch out for Pluto my dear. But you'll keep her won't you?

ZACHARY. *(Looks at Poe.)* How can I refuse her? *(WIFE kisses Zachary and exits door.)* Edgar, shall we continue?

POE. Yes. *(Pause, collecting himself to tell the story.)* However after several years ...

ZACHARY. Yes, Yes, Yes ... However *(Growing darker.)* ... after several years my general temperament and character, through the instrumentality of the fiend intemperance ... *(Pulls out bottle like a weapon, cat cries out, crossing to B, POE falls back on C.)*

POE. Ah!

ZACHARY. ...experienced a radical alteration for the worse. Drink? *(Crossing to Poe, offering bottle.)*

POE. No.

ZACHARY. Please. In the spirit of southern conviviality.

POE. *(Slowly take bottle and drinks.)* Ahhgh!

ZACHARY. *(THEY are at C.)* Not a good year but it has a jagged charm wouldn't you say?

POE. Yes. *(Drinks again.)*

ZACHARY. I grew day by day more moody, more irritable, more regardless of the feeling of others. *(Crossing to D.)*

POE. Yes, I know.

ZACHARY. *(Drunken.)* One night, returning home, much intoxicated from one of my haunts about town, I fancied the cat avoided my presence. *(ZACHARY approaches cat at B, cat moves away disgusted with Zachary.)* Come here Pluto. *(Cat refuses.)* Come here girl. *(Approaching to grab cat, before B, cat hissing throws off his hand scratching him.)* Ahhh! *(ZACHARY licks blood from hand, very dark.)* That wasn't very hospitable my pet. *(Cat issues small cry of fear realizing Zachary's transformation, avoids him as HE stalks her, crossing up stairs to A.)* Come here my pet ... *(Stalks, crossing to B, cat leaps off B to D.)* ... come here pretty girl.

POE. The fury of a demon instantly possessed him. *(ZACHARY pulls knife from pocket, unfolds it.)* A more than fiendish malevolence thrilled every fibre of his frame. *(ZACHARY leaps to D, grabs cat by throat, turning her upstage for a theatrical gouging out of Pluto's eye[9], to cat's cries of anguish.)* He deliberately cut one of its eyes from its socket.

(Cat runs off through doors A, doors remain open.)

ZACHARY. *(To Poe, apologetic, now sober and almost begging understanding.)* But you remember the cat did slowly recover.

POE. Yes, oh yes. *(Cat returns with eye patch to A.)*

ZACHARY. The socket of the lost eye presented, it is true, a frightful appearance. *(Cat hisses.)* But it no longer appeared to suffer pain. She went about the house as usual.

POE. But as might be expected fled in extreme terror on your approach. *(Cat hisses and shies from ZACHARY's approach to A.)*

ZACHARY. *(Very kindly.)* I had so much of my old heart left as to be at first grieved by this evident dislike from one who had once so loved me. *(Finally cat allows ZACHARY to pet her.)*

POE. But ...

ZACHARY. this ... *(Growing dark.)*

POE. feeling ...

ZACHARY. soon gave place...

POE. to irritation ... Then...

ZACHARY. came ...

POE. the spirit of ...

ZACHARY. *(Turns crossing to Poe at C.)* Perverseness! *(Drinks.)* One of the primitive impulses of the human heart.

POE. One of the indivisible primary faculties which give direction to the character of man. Who has not, a hundred times found himself committing a ...

ZACHARY. *(Collecting a rope with noose from behind doors at A.)* vile ...

POE. or a ...

ZACHARY. stupid ... *(Drinking.)*

POE. action, for no reason than because he knows he should not. *(Drinks.)*

ZACHARY. *(Chases cat to A, B, C, and grabs terrified cat at D hissing and scratching.)* One morning,

POE. In cold blood.

ZACHARY. *(Doing it as he speaks.)* I slipped a noose about its neck

POE. and hung it on the limb of a tree! *(Cat is "hung"[10] theatrically in doorway at A, by ZACHARY as OTHERS in black hoods "lift" cat so the hanging is not a realistic hanging. [Note: Pose featuring Zachary's hands on rope.])*

POE. Hung it with

POE & ZACHARY. tears

POE. streaming from his eyes. Hung it because he knew that she once

POE & ZACHARY. loved me,

POE. hung it *because* he knew that in doing so he was committing a sin.

ZACHARY. *(Running to Poe in terror.)* Help me please. *(Falling in his arms.)* Stop. No more. Please, I beg you. *(Hanging image dissolves. Hooded LIFTERS carry off cat and close doors.)*

POE. *(Inflamed with drink. Drinking.)* However one night as he sat half stupefied in a den of more than infamy, *(Pushing ZACHARY to turn and look as cat appears at B sitting on the shoulders of a hooded FIGURE in black, she now wears white gloves.)* His attention was suddenly drawn to some black object reposing upon the head of one of the immense hogsheads of gin. *(Cat purrs affectionately looking at Zachary, hands behind her.)*

ZACHARY. Pluto!
POE. No ...
ZACHARY. The eye!

(Hooded FIGURE carries cat to A.)

POE. No! Pluto had not a white hair upon any portion of her body. *(Cat reaches out white hand to Zachary.)*

ZACHARY. Her paws!!

POE. White! *(ZACHARY reaches to cat who "hops down" as "hogshead" bows out.)* Go on ... *(ZACHARY pets cat, cat purrs and rubs up against him in affectionate cat-like way.)*

ZACHARY. Barkeep, I'm going home. *(Tosses hooded FIGURE a coin, as ZACHARY leaves, cat pursues him to E, D, and G, over set, purring. HE occasionally stops to pet it.)*

When she reached the home she domesticated herself at once and immediately became a great favorite of my wife. *(At "home" cat plays with WIFE who enters A, cat crossing up to her, SHE pets it.)*

WIFE. What a lovely kitty. Look at those paws. White as snow!

ZACHARY. Yes.

WIFE. We should keep her, she seems to need a home. *(Cat purrs and plays.)*

ZACHARY. But, my dear. We haven't the time or patience to care for another ...

WIFE. Nonsense. How much bother can she be. *(To cat.)* Let me get you a nice bowl of milk. *(WIFE exits through doors and closes them.)*

POE. He soon found a ... *(Cat snakes around ZACHARY at G.)*

ZACHARY. dislike ... *(ZACHARY crosses to C, sits on platform.)*

POE. rising within him. With his aversion to her however, her partiality to him seemed to increase. Where ever he sat ... *(ZACHARY sits, cat curls in his lap.)* If he rose to walk ... *(ZACHARY walks away to D, cat chases him, becomes entangled in his footsteps, making him tumble, cat wraps arms about him affectionately at D.)* At such times, although he longed to

ZACHARY. Destroy it with one blow ...

POE. He yet withheld himself from doing so partly by a ...

ZACHARY. memory of my former crime ...

POE. But, confess, chiefly because ...

ZACHARY. *(Standing, running from cat a few steps, cat crosses to A, finds "yarn.")* Because I dreaded the beast ...

because, at times, its paws, its white white ... hands *(Cat plays with an oversized bundle of yarn. Slowly, cat stands playing with yarn.)* By slow degrees in moments of innocent play ...
POE. What? Tell us.
ZACHARY. An image I shudder to name.
POE. Tell us!

(Cat tosses yarn over door holding one end, strikes pose exactly like Zachary pulling rope of hanging.)

ZACHARY. There! Am I mad? Mad with dread, with terror, with evil! My hands on the gallows rope!
POE. *(Mocking.)* No, you're imagining.
ZACHARY. *(Crossing to Poe at C.)* No. Oh the mournful and terrible engine of horror and of guise of agony and of death! *(POE gives him drink, cat tosses yarn off crossing to B.)* Evil thoughts became my sole intimates. The darkest and most evil of thoughts. One day *(Cross to D then A.)* she accompanied me upon a household errand into the cellar of our old house. *(ZACHARY descends stairs, from A to C to before C, cat pursues him, becomes tangled in his legs, HE falls, cat smiles and purrs over him.)*
WIFE. *(Enters from above at doors as though upstairs, unable to see the "cellar.")* What *was* that? Did you fall? Are you all right?

(ZACHARY consumed with rage grabs an ax from behind wall at C, swings it down on cat, misses, loud crash of ax.)

WIFE. What's happening down there? *(Another swing of ax, which narrowly misses cat, who seems delighted with game, WIFE descend stairs to C̲, sees ZACHARY try to kill cat.)* My God! Stop this. Stop!

(ZACHARY misses again, cat poses near wall at H̲, ZACHARY cocks for enormous killing stroke, WIFE runs between cat and Zachary, SHE embraces cat and takes her behind wall at H̲ for shelter. ZACHARY madly swings ax. We hear THUD, WIFE screams in agony! HE swings again blind with rage, THUD, another scream. ZACHARY swings again and hits as cat slinks smiling out. Wife's white gloved hands reach from behind wall now drenched in blood as ZACHARY hits and hits and hits his target. Cat removes white gloves and exits, through A̲ closing doors.)

POE. No! No more. Stop, Stop! *(Runs to stop Zachary, POE is caught by MORAN and NURSES and is dragged screaming to bed that NURSES have brought on as ZACHARY exits, THEY strap him in as his rage fades to whimpers.)*

MORAN. This condition of sometimes violent fits continued for a period of thirteen to fourteen hours followed by what can only be described as ...

(NURSES flank bed, MORAN U. of bed, POE's head hangs off bed D. in blank glare.)

NURSE 1. *(POE in death-like trance.)* Mr. Poe?

(Pause.)

NURSE 2. Mr. Poe ...

(Pause.)

MORAN. Mr. Poe? *(HE taps medical record.)* Catalepsy. *(THUNDER is heard, taps record again, this turns into tapping of Raven outside.)*

(Title appears.)

"THE RAVEN"

(Tapping THUNDER, light of LIGHTNING showing through door windows—exact repetition of opening tableau—plus POE on bed, CHORUS flanks set.)

POE. *(Whispering.)* Presently my soul grew stronger, hesitating then no longer.
POE & CHORUS. *(Whispered by chorus, fearful.)* Sir.
POE. Said I,
POE & CHORUS. *(Whispered by CHORUS.)* Or madam truly your forgiveness I implore;
POE. but the fact is I was napping and so gently you came.
CHORUS & POE. *(Whispered by CHORUS.)* Rapping
POE. and so faintly you came
CHORUS & POE. *(Whispered by CHORUS.)* Tapping
POE. Tapping at my chamber door that I scarce was sure I heard you

(Pause, POE rises from bed, which is rolled off by NURSES and MORAN, THEY join flanking chorus, crosses to doors at A.)

POE. Here I opened wide the door ... *(Opens doors in fear, it RAINS.)* Darkness there and nothing more *(Closes door, RAIN, THUNDER, returns to D.)* Back into my chamber turning, all my soul within me.

(ALL the following chorus lines are whispered.)

POE & CHORUS. Burning ... *(Pause.)*

(TAPPING breaks pause.)

POE. Soon again I heard a
POE & CHORUS. Rapping
POE. Somewhat louder than before surely,
CHORUS. said I
POE. Surely, that is something at my window lattice. Let me see then what there is at and this
POE & CHORUS. Mystery
POE. explore—*(Terror; TAPPING.)* Let my heart be still a moment and this
POE & CHORUS. Mystery

(Under POE as he speaks, CHORUS - Shhhhhhh.)

POE. explore—tis the Wind and nothing more *(TAPPING builds, sound of RAIN, crossing to A open doors.)* Open here I fling the shutter.

(WIND, THUNDER, LIGHTNING "Raven"[11] enters [man on shoulders of another with wings made by fabric on poles held by arms, support actor wears half mask of Pallas] standing at A with wings out stretched to B and C.)

POE. *(Falling back to D.)* When with many a
POE & FEMALES. flirt
POE. and
POE. & MALES. flutter
POE. In there stepped a stately
POE & CHORUS. *(Forte.)* Raven
POE.
O'the saintly day of yore
Not the least observance made he
Not a minute stopped or stayed he
But with men of lord or lady
Perched above my chamber door
   POE & CHORUS. *(CHORUS in sotto voce.)*
Perched upon a bust of PALLAS just above my chamber door.

(The following lines are said in full voice.)

   CHORUS (1). Perched
   CHORUS (2). and
   CHORUS (3). sat
   CHORUS (4). and
   CHORUS. *(Whispered.)* Nothing more

(THUNDER - RAIN.)

   POE.
Then this ebony bird beguiling my sad fancy into smiling
By the grave and stern decorum of the countenance it wore.
   POE & CHORUS (1). *(Whispered by 1.)* Though thy crest
be shorn and shaven thou
   CHORUS. I said

POE & CHORUS (1). *(Whispered by 1.)* Are sure no craven. Ghastly grim and ancient raven wandering from the nightly shore—Tell me what thy lordly name is on the nights Plutonian shore!

POE. Quoth the Raven

CHORUS. Nevermore. *(Forte. Sound of RAIN.)*

POE. But the raven sitting lonely on the placid bust spoke only that one word, as if his

POE & CHORUS. *(Whispered by chorus.)* soul

(The following lines are whispered by all.)

POE & CHORUS (3). in that one word he did out pour

POE & CHORUS (4). Nothing further then he uttered

POE & CHORUS (4) & (1). Not a feather then a fluttered

POE & CHORUS (1) & (3) & (4). Till I scarcely more than muttered

POE & CHORUS (1). *(POE is full voiced; CHORUS (1) is whispered.)* Other friends have flown before—On the morrow *he* will leave me as my hopes have flown before. Then the bird said

CHORUS. *(Forte.)* Nevermore

(Sound of RAIN. On cue in line CHORUS becomes "cushioned seat"[12] for POE who faces the RAVEN U. as "CHORUS/CHAIR" continues to recite.)

POE. *("Sitting" in "seat" at E.)* But the Raven still beguiling all my fancy into smiling, straight I wheeled a cushioned seat in front of bird, and bust on door, Then upon the velvet sinking, I betook myself thinking fancy unto fancy, thinking what this ominous bird of yore

(The following lines by CHORUS are in full voice.)

    POE. What this
    CHORUS (1). grim
    CHORUS (2). ungainly
    CHORUS (3). ghastly
    CHORUS (4). gaunt and ominous
    POE & CHORUS. bird of yore
    POE. meant in croaking
    CHORUS. Nevermore

(Sound of RAIN. Reading accelerates as RAVEN approaches Poe slowly.)

    POE.
This I sat engaged in guessing, but no syllable expressing
To the fowl whose fiery eyes now
    POE & CHORUS. burned
    POE. into by bosom's core
    POE & CHORUS. *(Whisper building to forte.)*
This and more I sat divining with my head at ease reclining,
On the cushions velvet lining that the lamplight gloated 'ore.
    VIRGINIA. *(Enters at E.)* Eddy!

(Shatters the gloomy mood, LIGHTS up, RAVEN, CHAIR, exit as though a dream dissolves, leaving POE at E & VIRGINIA alone. VIRGINIA holds wildflowers.)

    POE. Virginia—my dearest ... cousin.

(SHE approaches him at E slowly reaching to him, then suddenly lunges tagging him playfully and running away to D.)

VIRGINIA. Tag, you're it *(Laughs.)*
POE. Oh, Virginia ....
VIRGINIA. Come on Eddy, let's play.
POE. Virginia *(Catching her infectious laughter.)* I would love to, *(Crossing to her at D.)* but I'm writing a ...
VIRGINIA. Oh I banish all gloomy stories from your mind. *(Tosses flowers at him playfully.)* It's a beautiful day, no demons in this field, come on *(Grabs his hand and dances him around.)* You're my favorite dancing partner.
POE. *(Playful as well.)* I'm disarmed with your flattery, mademoiselle.
VIRGINIA. *(With curtsy.)* Enchanté, Monsieur. *(THEY laugh.)*
POE. Virginia.
VIRGINIA. Yes Eddy.
POE. I want to tell you something,
VIRGINIA. You know Eddy, I love you ...
POE. Yes?
VIRGINIA. When you look at me with those sad eyes, you look like a puppy dog. Come on. *(Pulling him by his hand, trying to run off, runs into MRS. CLEMM at E.)* Oh, Mommy! *(Pecks her on cheek.)* I'll beat you to the top of that hill, come on! *(Runs off.)*
POE. Mrs. Clemm.
MRS. CLEMM. Yes, Edgar.
POE. I have to speak with you about Virginia ....
MRS. CLEMM. Edgar, I can see that ...
POE. I ... love ... Virginia. Passionately, devotedly.

MRS. CLEMM. Yes, I know. But Edgar, she is very young.

POE. I have been dreaming every day and night of the rapture I should feel in calling her my ... wife.

MRS. CLEMM. But Edgar, you are related ... cousins.

POE. *(Not listening.)* I have procured a sweet little house in a retired situation on church hill ...

MRS. CLEMM. Edgar, please, listen to me. I love you as dearly as I love her and nothing would make me happier.

POE. Then you ...

MRS. CLEMM. She's all I have in this world.

POE. Yes I know, but you would live with us and I could...

MRS. CLEMM. Please Edgar. *(Crosses to Poe at D, embraces him.)* Let me think on it. *(Kisses his cheek.)*

POE. All right.

(MRS. CLEMM exits.)

"ANNABEL LEE"

(Sound of SEASHORE under poem, VIRGINIA dances poetically around POE at D, to the recitation of poem, CHORUS enters and sits on flanks of set casually.)

CHORUS (1). It was many and many a year ago

CHORUS. *(Hushed.)* In a kingdom by the sea

CHORUS (2). That a maiden there lived whom you may know by the name of ...

CHORUS & POE. *(Hushed.)* Annabel Lee *(SHE moves, plays music, harp.)*

CHORUS (1). And this maiden she lived with no other thoughts than

POE. to love *(CHORUS.)* and be loved by me.
CHORUS (2). She was a child and I was a child
CHORUS. *(Hushed.)* In this kingdom by the sea.
CHORUS (2) but we
CHORUS. *(Hushed.)* loved
CHORUS (2). with a
CHORUS. *(Hushed.)* love
CHORUS (2). that was
CHORUS. *(Hushed.)* more than love
POE. I and my
POE & CHORUS. *(Hushed.)* Annabel Lee
POE. With a love that the winged seraph of heaven coveted her and me. *(THEY embrace at D.)*

(Tableau as CHORUS transforms to GOSSIPS and gather menacingly at A hiding in scarves and shawls U.)

POE. My love, my dearest wife.
VIRGINIA. Eddy!
GOSSIPS (1). *(Clucking.)* It's scandalous.
GOSSIPS (2). Reprehensible.
GOSSIPS (3). A crime.
GOSSIPS (4). A sin.
GOSSIPS (2). She's a child.
GOSSIPS (3). Twelve years old and his cousin
GOSSIPS (1). And he's ... ah! Twice her age.
GOSSIPS (3). It should never have happened.
GOSSIPS (4). Never.
GOSSIPS (2). Never.
GOSSIPS (1). Never more in this town.
CHORUS. *(Whispered from all over the stage.)* Nevermore!

(Quick fade to BLACK.)

END OF ACT I

ACT II

(Exact image of end of Act I, SEA sounds, harp MUSIC minor mode, Chorus U., VIRGINIA hums to the music, POE stares, pen in hand.)

VIRGINIA. Eddy ... Eddy... *(Shaking him in jest.)* Mr. Poe, Mr. Poe!

(NURSES appear in distance, U.)

NURSE 1. *(Appears in chorus removing shawl.)* Mr. Poe ...
NURSE 2. *(Same as Nurse 1.)* Mr. Poe ...

(NURSES disappear into shawls.)

POE. What ... Oh ... I'm sorry my dear ... another one of my ... stories.
VIRGINIA. *(Jesting.)*.Was it dull, dark
POE. Oh ...
VIRGINIA. soundless and melancholy *(Her laughs turn to a cough.)*
POE. Are you all right, my dear.
VIRGINIA. Yes ... don't mind me ... just the autumn air.
(SHE snuggles closer into him and closes her eyes, POE stares off and writes as HE speaks.)

POE. *(Writing—SHE rests in his lap.)* During the whole of a dull dark and soundless day in the autumn of the year, when the clouds hung

CHORUS & POE. *(Whispered by CHORUS.)* oppressively ...

POE. ... low in the heavens, I had been passing alone on horse back through a singularly dreary tract of country and at length found myself, within view *(Seeing it—rising to peer at it.)* of the ...

CHORUS & POE. *(Whispered by CHORUS.)* Melancholy.

POE. House of Usher—

(SOUND cue.)

VIRGINIA. *(In a sudden attack.)* Ahhh—Eddy, help me Eddyyyyy! *(SHE falls gagging—POE runs to her and SHE falls limp—bleeding at the mouth.)*

POE. Virginia, Virginia. *(No answer, SHE seems dead.)* Doctor! Call for a Doctor

(ALL whispered.)

    CHORUS (1). *(Desperate.)* Doctor
    CHORUS (2). *(Desperate.)* Doctor!
    CHORUS (3). *(Desperate.)* Doctor!
    CHORUS (4). *(Building.)* Doctor!
    CHORUS (5). *(Shrieked.)* Doctor!

(CHORUS 6 emerges from shawl—a doctor—with surgical mask, crossing to them at D with two NURSES, checks

her life signs, finds none. Stands and looks at POE who is holding the lifeless body, shakes head "no" - MUSIC.)

POE. *(Crying.)* Nooooo!

(Enter RODERICK USHER, music.)

RODERICK. *(Emerges from chorus at A.)* The Lady Madeline *(Gesturing to Virginia.)* is no more.

(Title in.)

"THE FALL OF THE HOUSE OF USHER"

(Reliving her death in horror, MUSIC.)

POE. The disease of the Lady Madeline Usher, Roderick Usher's only sister, had long baffled the skill of her physicians.
DOCTOR. *(HE removes mask.)* A settled apathy, a gradual wasting away of the person until ... catalepsy.
POE. Catalepsy!
RODERICK. *(Crossing down to D to pick up Madeline/Virginia.)* Hitherto she had steadily bourn up against the pressure of her malady, but finally she had succumbed.
POE. But are you certain she is *dead.*

(DOCTOR and NURSES exit, CHORUS exits.)

RODERICK. Come, we must preserve her body for a fortnight—in the family vaults below the walls.

POE. But Roderick—
RODERICK. *(Commanding through his grief.)* Come, I will need your help.

(RODERICK picks up Madeline/Virginia and exits doors at A. POE follows him and at the doors turns at A to describe the burial. CHORUS reenters flanking set.)

POE. I personally aided him in ...
POE & CHORUS. *(CHORUS whispered.)* ... the entombment ...
POE. The vault in which we placed the body was small, damp and entirely without means of admission of light, lying at great ...
POE & CHORUS. *(CHORUS whispered.)* ... depth.

(RODERICK returns, enters at B.)

POE. And now, some days of bitter grief having elapsed an observable ... change came over him. It seemed his mind was laboring with some oppressive ...
POE & CHORUS. *(Whispers.)* ... secret.
RODERICK. *(Starting.)* Ahh —no!
POE. My Friend!
RODERICK. Not a word. *(Listening to something.)*
POE. But Roderick ...
RODERICK. Not a Sound! *(Listening horrified, exits.)*
POE. His condition terrified, infected me. On the night of the eighth day after placing the lady Madeline in the tomb.

(THUNDERSTORM suddenly begins, though muffled by the closed windows.)

POE & CHORUS. Sleep

POE. *(Crossing to D.)* came not near my couch, irrepressive tremor listen! What can it be?! Certain low and indefinite sounds came through pauses in the storm *(HE listens—we hear these SOUNDS through the storm.)*

RODERICK. *(Suddenly bursting in at B seemingly from nowhere, raving in near lunacy.)* And have you not seen?

POE. Roderick!

RODERICK. You have not seen it? But stay, you shall *(Crossing to open windows at D before Poe, enormous crack of LIGHTNING and THUNDER.)*

RODERICK. Look!

POE. My god!!

CHORUS (2). The trees.

CHORUS (3). The rocks.

CHORUS (4). The lawn.

POE. They glow in an unnatural light.

CHORUS. They glow!

RODERICK. All terrestrial objects luminous by the gaseous exhalation from the *House of Usher*.

POE. Roderick, you must not, you shall not behold this! *(Closes window.)* These appearances are merely electrical phenomenon, not uncommon. Sit down. *(Seats him on C gets a preset.)* Here is one of your favorite romances. I will read and you shall listen.

CHORUS (1). Listen ...

CHORUS (2). Listen ...

CHORUS (3). Listen ...

CHORUS (4). Listen ...

RODERICK. Ahh! *(Low SOUND.)*[13]

POE. *(Sits on stairs of C, reads from a book.)* and so we will pass away this terrible night together. "And Ethebred waited no longer to hold parley with the hermit, uplifted his mace outright and with blows ripped and tore all asunder the door" *(SOUND with THUNDER.)* "But the good champion Ethebred entering within the door was amazed to perceive a ...

POE & CHORUS. *(Full.)* ... dragon ...

POE. ... of a scaly and prodigious demeanor *(SOUND louder, with fainter THUNDER.)* And Ethebred uplifted his mace and struck upon the head of dragon which gave up a ...

POE. & CHORUS. *(full.)* ... shriek ...

(Muffled shrieks by CHORUS.)

POE. ... so horrid and harsh.

(SOUND dominant over thunder.)

RODERICK. Now hear it! Yes, I hear it, and have heard it. Long, long, long, many minutes, many hours, many days, have I heard it—yet I dared not—oh pity miserable wretch that I am. I dared not, I *dared* not speak. *We have put her living in the tomb!* *(THUNDER.)*

CHORUS. *(Forte.)* Buried alive.

POE. Nooooo!

(STORM, THUNDER.)

RODERICK. I now tell you that I heard her first feeble movements in the hollow coffin, I heard them, many many days ago. Yet I dared not—I dared not speak. Oh wither shall I

fly! *(Stands.)* Will she not be here anon. Is she not hurrying to upbraid me for her haste.
CHORUS (1). *(Full.)* haste!
CHORUS (2). *(Full.)* haste!
CHORUS (3). *(Forte.)* haste!
CHORUS (4). *(Forte.)* haste!
RODERICK. Have I not heard her foot step on the stair *(Indicates doors at A. THUNDER—HEARTBEATS—MOANS.)* Do I not distinguish that heavy and horrible beating of her heart?
CHORUS (2). *(Full.)* her heart ...
CHORUS (3). *(Full.)* her heart ...
CHORUS (4). *(Forte.)* heavy ...
CHORUS (1). *(Forte.)* horrible ...
CHORUS *(Forte.)* Beating!
POE. *(Rises, tries to calm him.)* Roderick stop.
RODERICK. Madman! *(Throws him to floor at E, runs to stairs at A.)* I tell you that she now stands with out the door.

(Doors burst open—MADELINE[14]—in Death mask, blood on her white robes, hair wild, hands huge. CHORUS screams collectively.)

MADELINE. *(Shrieking.)* Roderick!!
CHORUS. *(Echoing.)* Roderick!!

(MADELINE descends on Roderick. Large extended SOUND cue as House of Usher falls. Fade to BLACK except pool of LIGHT on POE at E.)

POE. *(Distant RUMBLES. At E, in pool of LIGHT DL, HE writes.)* From that mansion I fled aghast—I turned—I saw the mighty walls of the House rushing asunder. There was a long tumultuous shouting sound like the voice of a thousand waters and the deep and dank tarn at my feet closed sullenly and silently over the fragments of the ...

POE & CHORUS. *(Whispered.)* ... House of Usher.

VIRGINIA. *(Weakly, from behind Poe, LIGHTS up, sunny, she looks radiant, at the doors with a DOCTOR and NURSE at her side.)* Eddy!

POE. Virginia!

(THEY run to one another.)

VIRGINIA. The doctor says I'm going to live.

POE. But the bleeding?

DOCTOR. *(Joining them at D.)* It was a blood vessel in her throat that burst. She should be fine Mr. Poe. Make sure she gets rest.

POE. I thought you were ... I feared ... you had left me.

(DOCTOR and NURSES exit.)

VIRGINIA. No Eddy, I would never leave you. *(Suddenly playful.)* Ha-ha, you and you're morbid poetry. Ha! Ha!

POE. Oh Virginia, don't mock me, please.

VIRGINIA. I better watch out or you'll have me pronounced dead next time I get the sniffles ...

POE. *(Catching her infectious impishness.)* Ha-ha, please Virginia.

(CHORUS joins laughter.)

VIRGINIA. ... and have me buried alive ha ha ha!

(General laughter by CHORUS, gibing POE, all happy that Virginia is still with them. CHORUS filters off laughing—VIRGINIA last. POE still jocular crossing to writing desk at G.)

CHORUS. *(Various voices improv lines.)* Buried alive, Ha! Did you hear that! Watch out Edgar! Be careful!

(Writing desk to G.)

POE. *(At G.)* Ha Ha! To be buried alive. *(Thinks—still impishly imagining, picks up quill at writing desk, composing, searching, writing.)* ... to be buried while alive is ... hmmm *(Calls into wings.)* Excuse me.
ALLOUISIUS. *(From offstage.)* Huh? Yes?

(POE gestures ALLOUISIUS to "come on." Enter Allouisius to D—a comic creation, priggish, smarmy, shy, but adamant about his fears, ambitiously affected in his dress. POE hands him the page, ALLOUISIUS reads.)

ALLOUISIUS. Oh my! *(Attempts to leave.)*
POE. *(Stopping him at E, as though his voice is a thread holding him on stage.)* Ah-a-a-a! Please Allouisius, hold forth. *(POE gestures causing LIGHT change.)*

(Title in.)

"THE PREMATURE BURIAL"

ALLOUISIUS. *(Striking a pose, committed to the enlightenment of his audience.)* There are certain themes of which the interest is all absorbing but which are too entirely horrible for the purposes of ... *(Looks to Poe.)*

POE. ... legitimate fiction. Go on Allouisius.

ALLOUISIUS. To be buried while alive is, beyond question the most terrific of these extremes which has ever fallen to the lot of mere mortality. That it has frequently, *very* frequently, so fallen can scarcely be denied. One of these very remarkable circumstances may be fresh in your memories. It occurred not very long ago in the neighboring city of Baltimore. The wife of one of the most respectable citizens was seized with a sudden and unaccountable illness.

ALLOUISIUS. *(Offstage SHRIEKS then THUD.)* She presented all the ordinary appearances of death. *(LIGHTS up in C.)* The lady was deposited in her family vault. *(Dies irae to the putting of coffin in vault by hooded MONKS, THEY close the door behind them.)* Within two days of her entombment ... *(Lid of coffin opens.)*

WOMAN *(Yawning.)* Ahh—Hubert? *(Calling.)* Oh Hubert could you order breakfast for me here in my room ... Hubert? *(SHE sits up, discovers, looks at audience.)* Oh dear!

ALLOUISIUS. Thus she remained and thus she rotted.

WOMAN. EEEEEKK!

(BLACKOUT.
LIGHTS up in area B.)

ALLOUISIUS. True, I swear, in the year 1810 a case of living inhumation happened in France *(MUSIC—Frere Jaques.)* The heroine of our story is ...

VICTORINE. *(French accent. At B.)* Je m'apelle Mademoiselle Victorine La Fourcarde.
ALLOUISIUS. A young woman of great personal *beauty*.
VICTORINE. *(Laughter.)* Merci.
ALLOUISIUS. possessing numerous suitors.
VICTORINE. *(As the SUITORS enter at B.)* Bonjour Jean, Bonjour Phillipe, *(Lovingly.)* Bonjour Antoine, *(Enter BANKER clearly very rich.)* Bonjour Monsieur Ronetelle *(SHE crosses to him.)*
ALLOUISIUS. She married the Banker Ronetelle for money, not love. *(Exit other SUITORS.)* After marriage, this gentleman neglected and ill-treated her. Having passed with him some wretched years ...
VICTORINE. Yuuukkk!!
ALLOUISIUS. She died
VICTORINE. *(SHE dies.)* Ahhh!
ALLOUISIUS. Or so was believed.
BANKER. Ahh! My sweet. *(Picks up hand, drops it— THUD.)* She has passed.

(Dies irae, as SHE is buried in a trap on B, ALL exit.)

ALLOUISIUS. Filled with despair one of her suitors journeyed to the grave with the romantic purpose of disinterring the corpse and possessing himself of her luxuriant tresses.

(Enter ANTOINE at __B__, with scissors—secretly opens grave, sees her, struck by his still burning love.)

ANTOINE. Ah, my Victorine, My love.
ALLOUISIUS. But to his amazement ...
VICTORINE. *(Leaping from grave.)* My Antoine! My love! Antoine—Allons! *(Kisses him, THEY close the grave and exit stealthily.)*
ALLOUISIUS. She fled with her lover to America. Twenty years later they returned to France.

(Re-enter at __B__ ,VICTORINE and ANTOINE, THEY have different hats.)

VICTORINE. Oh Antoine, are you sure he will not recognize me?
ANTOINE. My love, the years have so altered us our dearest friends will not know us.

(Enter BANKER and OTHERS, around __B__.)

ALL. Look, it's Victorine and Antoine! Antoine and Victorine—Merde!
BANKER. You are *my* wife, come with me. *(Grabs her—SHE resists.)*
VICTORINE. No No NO!
BANKER. Yes Yes Yes!

(Enter JUDGE to __B__.)

ALLOUISIUS. A judicial tribunal was convened.

(JUDGE wraps mallet, perhaps on Banker's head, calling tribunal tableau to be struck, it is struck.)

JUDGE. We find in favor of the young lady. Given the peculiar circumstances, the long lapse of years, we extinguish the authority of the husband.
BANKER. *Zut alors!*

(VICTORINE and ANTOINE raspberry at Banker.)

ALL. *Vive La France!*

(BLACKOUT.)

ALLOUISIUS. There is also, of course, the well-known case involving the use of the Galvanic Battery to revive the suppose dead which occurred in London in 1831.

(Dies irae as "corpse" is wheeled into room on "bed" to D. Three DOCTORS enter in white with battery.)

DOCTOR (1). Can *we* apply *the* electrodes now?!!!
DOCTOR (2). No No Desmond. We must first perform the post mortem. Howard.
DOCTOR (3). Yes Doctor.
DOCTOR (2). Scalpel.
DOCTOR (3). Scalpel.*(Slapping instrument in his hand.).*

(DOCTOR 2 "inserts" scalpel in abdomen[15] and begins to open "corpse.")

DOCTOR (1). Please, let me try my electrical experiment before any organs are removed.

DOCTOR (3). *(After looking at DOCTOR 2.)* Well all right Desmond. In the interest of science ... *(HE puts electrodes that look like giant barbecue tongs on head of corpse, throws switch, zapping SOUND. The CORPSE convulses and sits up, eyes open, knife sticking out of belly, groans as HE gets off table.)*

DOCTOR (1). My God.
DOCTOR (2). What is this.
DOCTOR (3). This is amazing!
CORPSE. *(Looks at them.)* Iy oth eeeeemd.
DOCTORS (1), (2), & (3). What?
CORPSE. Iyyee ood heen iyee ayiy!
DOCTOR (1). Did you understand?
DOCTOR (2). Not a word.
DOCTOR (3). Speak clearly.

(CORPSE starts charades, holds up three fingers.)

DOCTOR (2). Three words

(OTHERS chime in, yes, yes, yes, three. CORPSE puts fingers to nose and holds up one finger.)

DOCTOR (3). First word!

(CORPSE points to eye.)

DOCTOR (1). Eye!! Eye!!

(CORPSE points to nose, holds two fingers up.)

A MIDNIGHT DREARY

DOCTOR (2). Second word.

(CORPSE ties knot with gown, points to knot.)

DOCTOR (3). Gown.
DOCTOR (1). White.
DOCTOR (2). Knot! Knot! Knot!!!

(CORPSE points to nose.)

DOCTOR (3). Oh, I love this game!

(CORPSE pulls ear.)

DOCTORS (1), (2), & (3). Sounds like.

(CORPSE points to rolling bed.)

DOCTOR (3). Table
DOCTOR (2). Metal
DOCTOR (1). Cold

(CORPSE mimes sleeping.)

DOCTOR (2). Sleep
DOCTOR (3). Bed, Bed!!! I got it.
DOCTOR (1). I ... knot ... bed. I knot bed.
DOCTOR (2). Sounds like "bed" could be ... led
DOCTOR (3). Bread
DOCTOR (1). sled
DOCTOR (2). wed

DOCTOR (3). fed *(Victorious.)* I knot fed!

(CORPSE gags and falls, gags and falls.)

DOCTOR (1). Dead!!! I'm not dead!

(CORPSE points to nose, collapses backwards in fatigue, scalpel still sticking out of belly.)

DOCTORS (1), (2), & (3). I get it, I'm not dead! Good game!

(THEY cheer and clap. BLACKOUT.)

ALLOUISIUS. *(In pool of LIGHT at E.)* Indeed. It is a fact that such premature interments occur frequently without our cognizance. What I have now to tell is of my own actual knowledge, of my own positive and personal experience. *(Dark MUSIC.)* For several years I had been subject to attacks of the singular disorder which physicians have agreed to term catalepsy in default of a more definite title. Once having fallen into trance-like clutches of the disease the closest scrutiny, the most rigorous medical tests fail to establish any material distinction between the state of the sufferer and what we conceive of absolute death. This state can last for days, even weeks. Sometimes my fancy crew claimed I talked "of worms, of tombs, and epitaphs." I was lost in reveries of death and the idea of premature burial, held continual possession of my brain. Once me thought I was immersed in a catalytic trance of more than usual duration and profundity.

A MIDNIGHT DREARY

(ALLOUISIUS crosses to "bed," still at D lies down, dark low tones of MUSIC swell and fade off to silence.)

FIGURE (1). *(After a silence.)* Arise!

(Voices from hooded FIGURES are in distant shadows up stage on A and stairs before A.)

FIGURE 2). Arise!
FIGURE (3). Arise!
FIGURE (4). Arise!

(ALLOUISIUS sits erect. Hooded FIGURES approach him, grasp his wrists and bring him to standing as they speak.)

FIGURE (2). Arise!
FIGURE (3). Did I not bid thee ...
CHORUS. Arise!
ALLOUISIUS. And who art ... thou?
FIGURE (4). I have no name in the regions which I inhabit.
FIGURE (3). I was mortal ...
FIGURE (2). but am friend I was merciless ...
FIGURE (1). but am faithful. Dost thou feel that I ...
FIGURE (2). shudder. My teeth chatter as I ...
FIGURE (3). speak, yet it is not with the chilliness of the night.
FIGURE (4). How canst thou tranquilly sleep?
FIGURE (2). I cannot rest for the cry of *these* great agonies.
FIGURE (1). Get thee up.

(ALLOUISIUS off "bed" is rolled to the side.)

CHORUS. Behold. *(Pointing out over audience.)*

ALLOUISIUS. *(LIGHT and SOUND cue.)* I looked. The graves of all mankind had caused to be thrown open—from each issued the faint phosphoric radiance of decay!! But alas! The real sleepers were fewer by many millions than those who slumbered *not at all!* The feeble struggling—the melancholy rustling from the garments of the buried.

FIGURE (3). Is it not—

FIGURE (1). Oh, is it not a pitiful ...

FIGURE (2). sight!

CHORUS. *(Crescendo.)* Oh God, is it not a pitiful sight!

ALLOUISIUS. Ahhhh! *(Waking screaming—hooded FIGURES vanish.)* Mother! Father! Help, Help, Help! *(LIGHTS up, ALLOUISIUS clutches "bed.")*

(MOTHER and FATHER enter to D.)

MOTHER. What is it Allouisius??

FATHER. What's the trouble Allouisius?

ALLOUISIUS. *(Clutching them.)* Oh save me! Save me! *(Slowly fading from his terror.)* Save ... me ... oh sorry.

MOTHER. Did you have a bad dream?

ALLOUISIUS. Yes! Yes, that must have been it.

MOTHER. *(Holding him like a little boy.)* Poor baby.

FATHER. Allouisius, maybe we should take you to a doctor ...

ALLOUISIUS. No. No. I'm fine. Just fine. *(Suddenly passionate.)* Just promise me one thing.

FATHER. What?

MOTHER. What Allouisius?

ALLOUISIUS. Promise me you won't bury me until I'm dead, very dead. Stinky smelly dead!

FATHER. What are you ...

ALLOUISIUS. Just promise me please.

FATHER & MOTHER. *(After looking to each other.)* We promise not to bury you until you're dead.

ALLOUISIUS. Very dead.

FATHER & MOTHER. Very dead.

FATHER. *(Exiting, to mother.)* We have a very strange son.

MOTHER. Bizarre!

ALLOUISIUS. *(Smug.)* I entered into a series of elaborate precautions. Among other things I had the family vault so remodelled as to admit of being readily opened from within. There were arrangements also for free admission of air and light and convenient receptacles for food and water.

COFFIN MAKER. *(Entering to D.)* Excuse me sir.

ALLOUISIUS. Yes?

COFFIN MAKER. I finished the modifications you requested in your coffin.

ALLOUISIUS. Wonderful—let me see it.

(The coffin is imaginary, perhaps we hear sounds of things as the COFFIN MAKER demonstrates.)

COFFIN MAKER. Well, there she is! *(Gestures D. of D.)*

ALLOUISIUS. My, my, it's lovely.

COFFIN MAKER. You see it's warmly and softly padded.

ALLOUISIUS. Very nice.

COFFIN MAKER. And this lever here on the inside of the lid releases the latch and the springs will make the lid fly open even with the feeblest pressure.

ALLOUISIUS. Excellent.

COFFIN MAKER. And the hole is there you requested ... now what was that for? I've forgotten.

ALLOUISIUS. The bell rope.

COFFIN MAKER. Of course, of course. The bell rope. Well then if that's quite satisfactory, I'll be on my way.

ALLOUISIUS. Very satisfactory, thank you very much. *(Paying him.)*

COFFIN MAKER. Have a nice ... I mean I hope that ... Well goodbye.

ALLOUISIUS. Farewell. *(To audience.)* But alas! What avails the vigilance against the destiny of man? Not even these well contrived securities sufficed to save from uttermost agonies of living *inhumation. (SOUND.)*

ALLOUISIUS. There arrived an epoch, as often before there had arrived, in which I found myself emerging from total unconsciousness into the first feeble and indefinite sense of existence. I am cognizant that I am not awaking from ordinary sleep. I recollect that I have been subject to catalepsy. *(ALLOUISIUS has maneuvered himself into the bottom of "bed" at D and becomes his "coffin" now.)* I could not summon the courage to move. My shuddering spirit was overwhelmed by danger. Despair alone urged me after long irresolution to uplift the heavy lids of my eyes. It was dark! All dark! I endeavored to shriek, I could not. *(HE reaches up, feels the "coffin lid.")* Hardwood, not six inches from my face. Yes I repose within a coffin! *(Pushing on "lid.")* Open! Open! Damn you open. I can't find the lever. The bell rope where is it? Nothing. This coffin has no padding. What do I smell—the moist earth! Nooo! I am not within the family vault! I have fallen into a trance while absent from home! Among strangers!

A MIDNIGHT DREARY 59

ALLOUISIUS. They have buried me like a dog! Nailed up in some common coffin! Thrust deep, deep in some ordinary and nameless grave. Ah, help.
Ah, help. *(Pounding and shrieking.)*
SAILOR 1. Hello! Hello there.

(Sailors entering suddenly around "bed" at D.)

SAILOR 2. What the devil's the matter now?
SAILOR 3. *(Actor who played mother perhaps.)* Get out o that!
SAILOR 1. What do you mean by yowling in that eerie kind of style, like a catamount?

(SAILORS drag ALLOUISIUS out and sit him on "bed.")

ALLOUISIUS. Where am I? What's going on!?
SAILOR 2. Why you're on a boat on the St. James river.
SAILOR 1. Don't you remember?
ALLOUISIUS. Remind me.
SAILOR 3. You and yer friend were on a hunting trip.
ALLOUISIUS. Yes, yes, I remember that.
SAILOR 2. You were caught by a storm.
ALLOUISIUS. Yes, the storm.
SAILOR 1. And asked us for ...
ALLOUISIUS. Shelter on board your ship ...
SAILOR 3. So we put in these births
ALLOUISIUS. with no bedding.
SAILOR 2. Bedding, ha! No call for such thing on this boat.
ALLOUISIUS. And the dimensions of the birth are very like those of a ... of a ...

SAILOR 1. What?

ALLOUISIUS. Never mind. What is the smell of moist earth?

SAILOR 3. Our cargo of garden mulch.

SAILOR 2. We were unloading it when we heard your screamin!

ALLOUISIUS. *(Laughing madly.)* Ha Ha Ha, well thank you, thank you ... I mean I'm sorry to have disturbed you.

SAILOR 1. No trouble.

SAILOR 2. You settle down now.

SAILOR 3. Good night sir.

SAILOR 2. *(As THEY exit.)* That is one very strange passenger.

SAILOR 3. Bizarre!

(LIGHTS, happier MUSIC.)

ALLOUISIUS. *(Pushes "bed" off.)* Out of evil, proceeded good. After these vents, my soul acquired tone, acquired temper. I went abroad. Took vigorous exercise. Breathed the free air of heaven. I thought upon subjects other than death. I discarded my medical books. I read no "Night Thoughts," no fustian about church yards, no bugaboo tales *(Grabbing quill from Poe at G.)* such as this. In short I became a new man. I discussed forever my charmed apprehensions and with them vanished the cataleptic disorder of which they had been less the consequence than the cause.

(Enter MOTHER and FATHER.)

MOTHER. We still love you, Allouisius.

ALLOUISIUS. Thanks mum. *(Kiss, exit.)*

(MESSENGER comes to Poe. Solemnly gives him a message, POE reads it, grief envelopes him. HE exits with MESSENGER in haste. After THEY are gone NURSES roll covered corpse on to D. POE enters through doors up center at A. Slowly crossing DC to table with corpse. Lifts the sheet. It is Virginia. HE grieves. NURSES and DOCTOR exit. We hear the SEA and the HARP that played under "Annabel Lee" in Act I.)

(Title in.)

"ANNABEL LEE"

(A hushed performance of the end of the poem, CHORUS flanks set.)

CHORUS (2). And this is the reason that long ago
CHORUS. *(Whispered.)* In this kingdom by the sea.
CHORUS (2). A wind blew out of a cloud by night chilling my ...
CHORUS & POE. Annabel Lee. *(POE lifts her from table, places her on bier, CHORUS members carry her to B.)*
CHORUS (2). So that her high born kinsmen came and bore her away from me
CHORUS (3). to
CHORUS (4). shut
CHORUS (1). her
CHORUS (2). up
CHORUS (3). in a
CHORUS. Sepulcher. In this kingdom by the sea

(HARP out as she is placed in grave, trap on B.)

CHORUS (2). The angels, not half so happy in heaven, went envying her and me

CHORUS (4). Yes, that is the reason (as all men know.)

CHORUS. *(Whispered.)* In this kingdom by the sea.

CHORUS (2). That the wind came out of the cloud chilling and killing my Annabel Lee.

POE. But our

POE & CHORUS 1. Love it was stronger by far than the love of those who were older than we.

CHORUS (4). Of many far wiser than we ...

CHORUS (1) & CHORUS (2). and neither the angels in heaven above, nor the demons down under the sea, can ever dissever my soul from the soul of the beautiful

CHORUS. *(Whispered.)* Annabel Lee.

POE.

For the moon never beams without bringing me dreams of the beautiful Annabel Lee.

And the stars never rise but I see the bright eyes of the

beautiful Annabel Lee. And so all the night tide I lie down by
   the side of my darling,

my darling, my life and my bride.

In her sepulcher there by the sea.

CHORUS. In her tomb by the side of the sea.

(GOSSIPS gather on A some pose as end of act, POE at grave at B, dripping with sincere hypocrisy.)

GOSSIP (1). so ...
GOSSIP (2). so ...

A MIDNIGHT DREARY

GOSSIP (3). So ...
GOSSIP (4). So it ends.
GOSSIP (3). It's so sad.
GOSSIP (2). They loved each other so.
GOSSIP (1). I always felt they were a lovely couple, no?
GOSSIP (4). He's a changed man.
GOSSIP (3). Never be the same.
GOSSIP (1). *(Nipping.)* Perhaps it's just as well.

(POE crosses U. past gossips, turns, now at podium above them, THEY APPLAUD as if we are mid lecture.)

(Title in.)

"THE POETIC PRINCIPLE"

(POE at writing desk, now a podium for a lecture at A, APPLAUSE, HE speaks deeply moved with conviction.)

POE. Thus, I have endeavored to convey to you my conception of the Poetic Principle. The principle itself is strictly and simply the human aspiration for Syrenial Beauty. This principle is always found in due elevating excitement of the soul. The Poet recognizes the ambrosia which nourishes his soul, in the bright orbs that shine in heaven, in the volutes of the flower, in the waving of the grain fields, in the twinkling of half hidden brooks, in the star mirroring depths of lonely wells. He perceives it in the songs of birds, in the sighing of the night wind, in the surf that complains to the shore, in the voluptuous perfume of the hyacinth. In the suggestive odor that comes to him at eventide from the distant undiscovered islands over dim oceans. He owns it in all unworldly motives in all chivalrous generous and self-sacrificing deeds. He feels it in the beauty of women. In the grace of her step, in the lustre of her eye, in the melody of her voice, in her burning enthusiasms, in her gentle charities, but above all, ah far above all, he feels it in the altogether divine majesty of her love.

(THEY call Poe over to "bed" at D. The exact image of the first scene is recreated.)

Dr. MORAN. Mr. Poe ...
CHORUS. *(Flanking set, whispered.)* Poe.
NURSE 1. Mr. Poe ...
CHORUS. *(Whispered.)* Poe.
NURSE 2. Mr. Poe ...
CHORUS. *(Whispered.)* Pooooooooooee

(The RAVEN enters at A, looms above him. The DOCTOR and NURSES exit slowly, silence then ...)

POE. *(Struggling, dying.)* Then me thought the air grew denser, perfumed from an unseen censer. *(Enter dark angel with smoking censer[16].)* Swung by Seraphin whose footfalls tinkled on the tufted floor.
POE & CHORUS. *(To Raven, forte.)* Wretch
POE. I cried.
POE & CHORUS. *(Forte.)* Thy God hath lent thee

POE. By these angels he hath sent thee. Respite—Respite and nepenthe from thy memories of Lenore. *(Reaching to where she is about to appear.)*
VIRGINIA. *(At C.)* Eddy! Eddy ... goodbye

(POE reaching out to Virginia.)

POE. Quaff, oh quaff, this kind nepenthe and forget this lost Lenore.
VIRGINIA. *(Hushed.)* Quoth the Raven ...
CHORUS. *(Whispered.)* Nevermore!

(VIRGINIA vanishes, sound of RAIN.)

POE. Prophet
POE & CHORUS. *(Whispered.)* said I.
POE. Thing of evil, Prophet still if bird of devil. Whether tempter or whether tempest tossed thee here ashore. Desolate get all undaunted on this desert land enchanted. On this home by ...
POE & FULL CHORUS. *(Whispered.)* horror.
POE. haunted. Tell me truly I implore, Is there
POE & CHORUS (1). Is there balm in Gilead?
POE. tell me, tell me I implore. Allen, Quoth the Raven
CHORUS. *(Full.)* Nevermore.

(Sound of RAIN.)

POE. *(Shrieked.)* Be that word our sign in parting bird or fiend.
POE & CHORUS. *(Whispered.)* I shrieked upstarting

POE. *(Shrieked.)* Get thee back into the tempest and the nights Plutonian shore. *(THUNDER.)* Leave no black plume a token of that lie they soul hath spoken, Leave my loneliness unbroken *(Rising, standing on bed.)* quit the bust above my door.

(Crescendo and thunder, POE crosses up to A rips mask of Pallas away to reveal Death mask beneath.)

POE. Take thy beak from out my heart and take thy form from off my door.
BERTRAM. Quoth the Raven
CHORUS. *(Forte, POE stumbles to D, falls down on bed.)* Nevermore

(THUNDER, RAIN. RAIN slackens.)

POE. *(Collapsed, dying, hushed.)* And the Raven never flitting still is sitting still is sitting.

(HOODED IMAGES of death approach and hover, lay a hand on his chest, head, face, one by one through remaining text.)

POE. On the pallid bust of Pallas just above my chamber door, and his
POE & CHORUS. *(CHORUS whispered.)* Eyes
POE. have all the seeming of a
CHORUS. *(Whispered.)* Demon
POE. That is ...
CHORUS (1). Dreaming *(Hushed extended on sung high voice.)*

POE. *(Speaks, dreaming.)* And the *(Slow labored. Whispered.)* lamp light on him streaming throws his *(Deep note, hushed.)* Shadow on the floor. And my

POE & CHORUS. *(Whispered.)* soul

POE. from out that shadow that lies floating on the floor, shall be lifted *(Fading.)*

Chorus *(Hushed.)* Nevermore.

Dr. MORAN. *(In SPOTLIGHT.)* His last words were ...

POE. Lord help my poor soul *(HE dies.)*

(Tableau; POE expired with hooded FIGURE's hands on his chest, neck and face. RAVEN hovering above over death mask, suddenly silently hooded FIGURES and RAVEN exit. Enter MORAN D. in the glow of a pool of LIGHT.)

MORAN. This is as faithful an account as I am able to furnish for the record of the death of one Edgar A. Poe. *(Pause, exit, fade out on MORAN, fade to BLACK.)*

The End

Footnotes

[1] Chorus - Be creative in your use of these voices. Potentially a most haunting and powerful device in the production. Redistribute and re-orchestrate if you have the impulse. Use a choir master or musician as your assistant.

The numers 1,2,3,4 imply sections of the chorus divided by vocal range. For example:

Chorus 1 – Soprano
Chorus 2 – Tenor
Chorus 3 – Mezzo
Chorus 4 – Base/Baritone
Chorus – Meaning entire chorus.

[2] The Bed. (See picture p. 70.)

[3] Titles - Locates the action of the play in the fabric of specific stories by Poe. Could be projections, could be posters, could be optional.

[4] Writing desk. (See picture p. 71.)

[5] Bertram's Chains - The cuffs are oversized so they can easily be dropped from his hands on cue.

[6] Heartbeat and dismembering sounds - Can be created on a cued tape. Could be done live with a percussion device on stage (my preference)- a drum for heartbeat, a club in soggy rags for dismembering. Use your imagination.

[7] Body parts - If this becomes grotesquely comic, it's not awful. Poe did have a comic flair and the "relief" might amplify the horror of the finale.

[8] Pluto the Cat - A woman (or man) in blacks or a black leotard (if it looks "cat-like"). The actor "personifies" the cat theatrically and need not be "on all fours." Be creative.

9 Eye gouging - Should be masked and theatrical, holding cat U. of Zachary. No sharp objects should ever come near anyone's eyes.

10 Cat hang - Under no circumstances should the "cat" be really hung by the neck no matter how safe it may seem. The hang should be done with the noose "motivating" the death theatrically and all weight assumed by the hooded figures supporting the cat. The noose should be incapable of taking *any* weight for safety reasons.

11 The Raven. - (See picture p. 72.) The creation by four actors. Actor B with ravens mask or beak. Actor A with mask of PALLAS with skeleton death mask beneath. Actor's C and D as "rod puppeteers" working wings. Actor B is on actor A's shoulders.

12 Cushioned Seat - (optional). (See picture p. 73.) Actor A in a "stone" position folded in a deep kneel with head bowed and actor B and C kneeling upright, as "arms" of chair.

13 Have fun with this one. What is the sound of someone trying to escape from a tomb? Scraping? Low moans? Cries? Beating?

14 Madeline risen from the tomb - A very brief image could be created with a fright wig or an inexpensive joke shop mask. She must be able to get into it quickly and out of it more quickly.

15 Actor of "dead" man needs a "pillow" or a safe pad with impenetrable backing to accept and hold "scalpel" in the appropriately safe and comic manner.

16 Dark angel with censer - Be creative. (optional image).

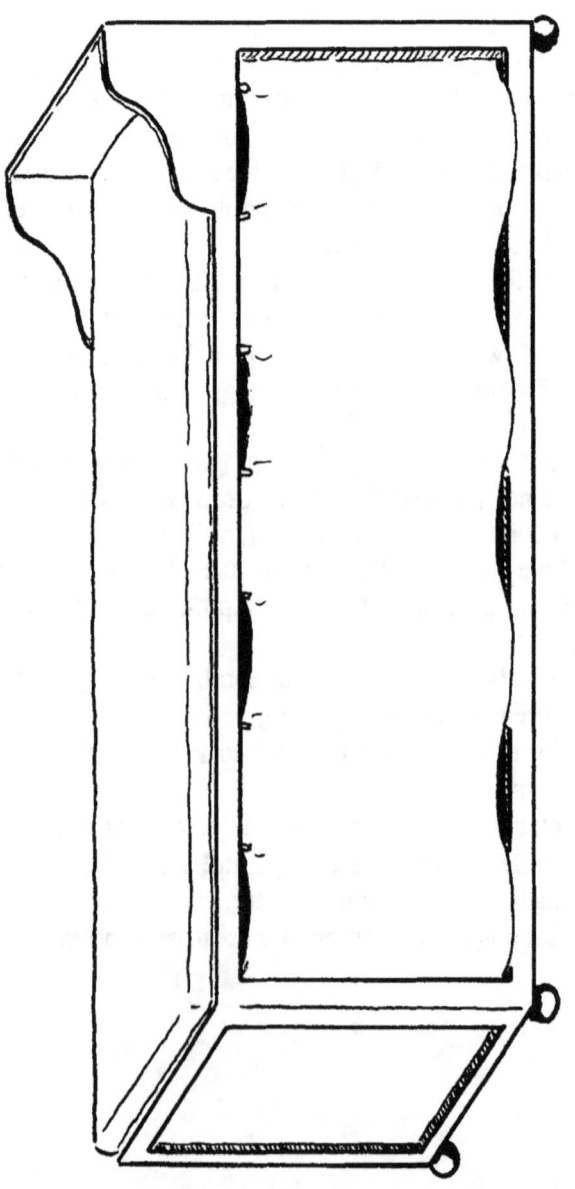

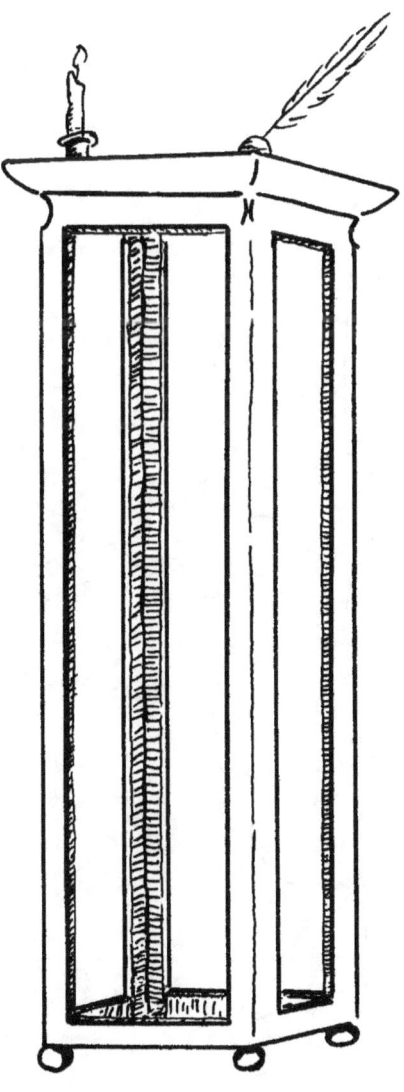

A MIDNIGHT DREARY

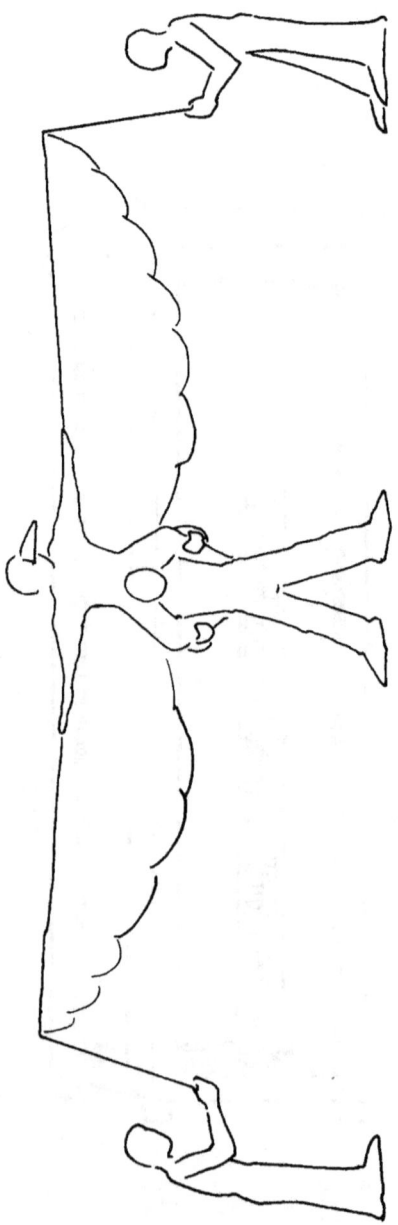

A MIDNIGHT DREARY

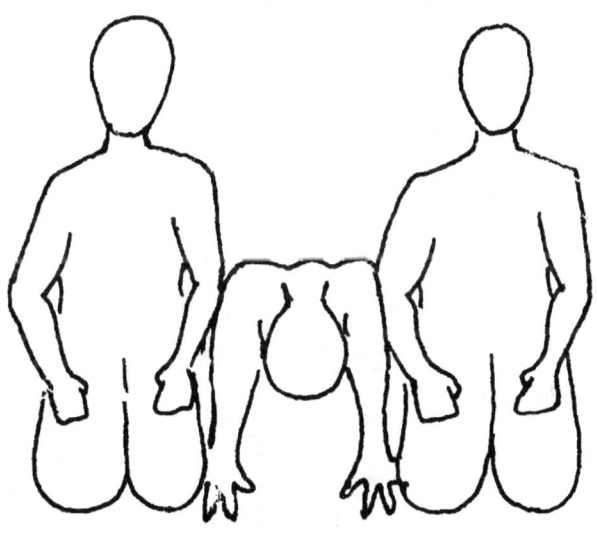

A MIDNIGHT DREARY

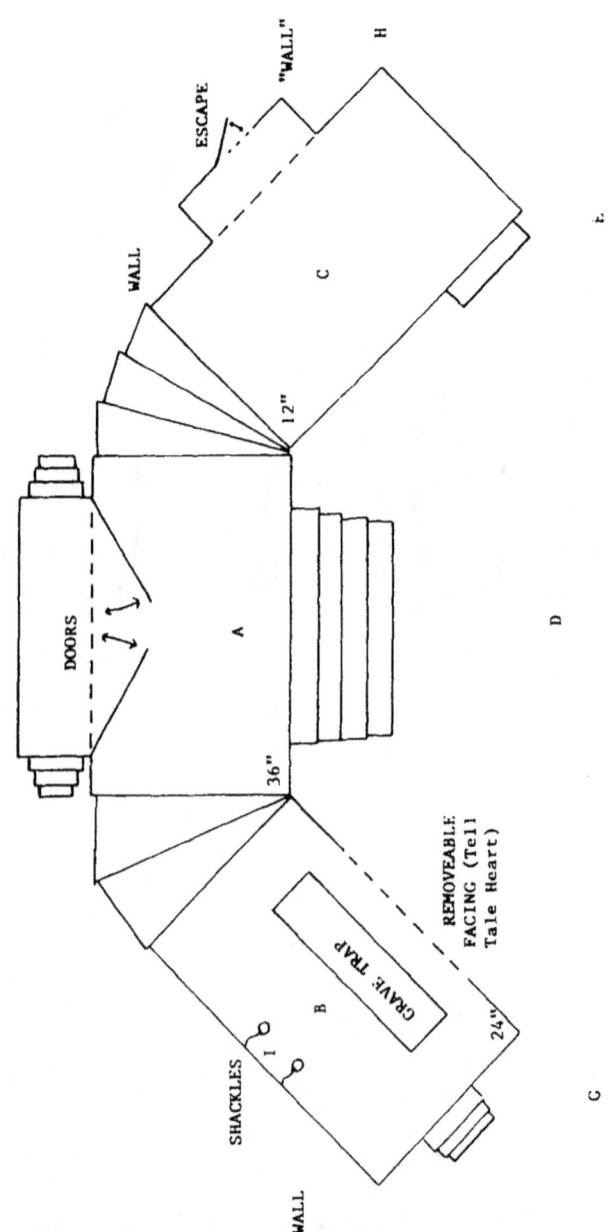

www.ingramcontent.com/pod-product-compliance
Lightning Source LLC
Chambersburg PA
CBHW052029290426
44112CB00014B/2441

www.ingramcontent.com/pod-product-compliance
Lightning Source LLC
Chambersburg PA
CBHW052029290426
44112CB00014B/2444